ECOLOGY WATCH

DESERTS

Clint Twist

D1502683

DILLON PRESS
NEW YORK

First American publication 1991 by Dillon Press, Macmillan Publishing Company, 866 Third Avenue, New York, NY 10022

Macmillan Publishing Company is part of the Maxwell Communication Group of Companies

First published by Evans Brothers Limited, 2A Portman Mansions, Chiltern Street, London W1M 1LE

Typeset by Fleetlines Typesetters, Southend-on-Sea
Printed in Spain by GRAFO, S.A. – Bilbao

Library of Congress Cataloging-in-Publication Data

Twist, Clint.
    Deserts / Clint Twist.
        p. cm. – (Ecology Watch)
    Includes index.
    Summary: A study of deserts, their climate, and the plants and animals that struggle to survive in this harsh environment.
    ISBN 0-87518-490-1
    1. Desert ecology – Juvenile literature. 2. Deserts – Juvenile literature. [1. Deserts. 2. Desert animals. 3. Desert plants. 4. Ecology.] I. Title. II. Series.
QH541.5.D4T85 1991
574.5'2652—dc20
                                        91–22471
                                            CIP
                                            AC

Acknowledgments

Editor: Su Swallow
Design: Neil Sayer
Production: Jenny Mulvanny

Illustrations: David Gardner, Graeme Chambers
Maps: Hardlines, Charlbury

For permission to reproduce copyright material the author and publishers gratefully acknowledge the following:

Cover (Monument Valley, Arizona, USA) Ronald Toms, Oxford Scientific Films
Title page (sand dunes, Australia) Otto Rogge, NHPA

p4 Richard Packwood, Oxford Scientific Films **p5** (left) Raimund Cramm, Bruce Coleman Limited, (right) Peter Davey, Bruce Coleman Limited **p7** Hutchison Library **p8** Dave Brinicombe, Hutchison Library **p9** Charles Henneghien, Bruce Coleman Limited **p10** (left) Christina Gascoigne, Robert Harding Picture Library, (right) Anthony Bannister, NHPA **p12** Anthony Bannister, NHPA, (inset) K H Switak, NHPA **p13** Carol Hughes, Bruce Coleman Limited **p14** Stan Osolinski, Oxford Scientific Films **p15** Sally Morgan/ECOSCENE **p16** (left) Jen and Des Bartlett, Bruce Coleman Limited, (top right) Owen Newman, Oxford Scientific Films, (bottom right) Ronald Toms, Oxford Scientific Films **p17** Stephen J Doyle, Bruce Coleman Limited **p18** K H Switak, NHPA **p19** Dr Eckart Pott, Bruce Coleman Limited **p20** Gerald Cubitt, Bruce Coleman Limited, (inset) David Hughes, Bruce Coleman Limited **p21** D V Matthews, NHPA **p22** (top left, center and bottom) David Thompson, Oxford Scientific Films, (right) Jane Burton, Bruce Coleman Limited **p23** (top) Densey Clyne, Oxford Scientific Films, (bottom) Jen and Des Bartlett, Bruce Coleman Limited **p24** K H Switak, NHPA **p25** K H Switak, NHPA **p26** Anthony Bannister, Oxford Scientific Films **p27** Carol Hughes, Bruce Coleman Limited **p28** G I Bernard, Oxford Scientific Films **p29** Konrad Whote, Bruce Coleman Limited **p30** (left) Eyal Bartov, Oxford Scientific Films, (right) M P L Fogden, Bruce Coleman Limited **p31** (top) Stan Osolinski, Oxford Scientific Films, (bottom) Mike Brown, Oxford Scientific Films, (inset) Jen and Des Bartlett, Bruce Coleman Limited **p32** Mickey Gibson, Oxford Scientific Films **p33** Anthony Bannister, NHPA **p34** Peter Johnson, NHPA **p35** Gerald Cubitt, Bruce Coleman Limited **p36** Prato, Bruce Coleman Limited **p37** Giorgio Gualco, Bruce Coleman Limited **p38** Hans Reinhard, Bruce Coleman Limited **p39** Anthony Bannister, NHPA **p40** Mark N Boulton, Bruce Coleman Limited **p41** Carol Hughes, Bruce Coleman Limited **p42** Sarah Errington, Hutchison Picture Library **p43** Derek Bayes, Aspect Picture Library **p44** (top) Eyal Bartov, Oxford Scientific Films, (bottom) Jeremy Hartley, Panos

Contents

Introduction

About one-seventh of the world's land surface is covered with deserts, areas that are too dry to be of any real importance to people. The driest deserts receive no rain at all for years at a time. Desert climate creates a very harsh environment, one in which the struggle for existence is never-ending, and life seems almost impossible. Yet deserts are far from being empty spaces. They have their own characteristic plant and animal wildlife that is woven together into a complex **ecosystem**. The ecosystem is simpler than those on other parts of the earth's surface, but it is more complicated than it may seem. Survival in the desert means adapting to desert conditions, and many desert plants and animals have adapted in ways that are not always obvious.

In some respects, the desert's harsh climate has worked to its advantage. Because conditions are so inhospitable for

▽ Deserts may look lifeless at midday, but all kinds of animals emerge as the sun goes down.

▽ This spiny-tailed lizard lives in the Sahara.

whole in order to understand how the individual pieces work and how they fit together. It is only by continuing to study the ecology of the deserts that we stand any chance of limiting their growth, let alone of turning them into productive land.

▽ The prickly pear cactus grows wild in deserts in the United States and Mexico, but people have taken it to other parts of the world.

human beings, the desert ecosystem is largely unspoiled by human interference. Most of the world's deserts remain true wildernesses, and apart from a few instances of greed and shortsightedness, human activity does not threaten the desert ecosystem. In fact, quite the opposite is true: Human activity positively encourages the desert ecosystem.

Deserts form as a result of the world's climate system, a process which may take millions of years. But once a desert has become established, it takes very little encouragement to make it expand quite rapidly. Little human activity takes place in the heart of the desert, because human population is clustered around the edges, where conditions are slightly more favorable. Unfortunately, taking advantage of these favorable conditions often means upsetting the balance of nature. **Overgrazing** by herds and flocks of domestic animals can quickly turn the semidesert at the fringes into real desert. Our planet already has more than enough desert, and the gradual expansion of these wildernesses through **desertification** is now a worldwide problem.

In some parts of the world, ambitious **irrigation** schemes are threatening the deserts' precious reserves of water in an attempt to produce more food. In the short term, these irrigation schemes may turn the deserts green, but the long-term consequences may be to make the deserts much drier.

One of the great values of **ecology** is that it teaches us to look at an environment as a

ecosystem—a large self-contained community of plants and animals inhabiting the same environment.
overgrazing—the process by which animals eat so much vegetation that the plants are destroyed.
desertification—the process by which land at the edges of a desert turns into desert.
irrigation—any method for supplying additional water to crops and fields.
ecology—the study of the relationships among plants, animals, and their environment.

Deserts and droughts

Desert conditions

A desert is an area of land suffering from almost permanent drought. Although deserts may differ in other respects, all deserts have this factor in common: Water, which is essential for life, is in very short supply.

The average rainfall in desert areas is less than four inches per year. In the driest places, for example in Chile's Atacama Desert in South America, no rain has fallen during the last 40 years. Most deserts, however, do receive some rainfall, usually as sudden storms which occur during one or two months in the year. Lack of rainfall is only part of the story. The air in deserts has very low humidity—the air is very dry and contains little water vapor.

The absence of moisture in the air above deserts means that clouds are rare, and most deserts have completely cloudless skies throughout the year. As a result, the air and the land surfaces are exposed to the full heating effect of direct sunlight. While the sun is shining, the air temperature regularly reaches 105°F, and may even climb as high as 120°F. The land itself gets even hotter: The surface temperature of sand and rocks can reach 165°F during the hottest part of the day.

At night, however, the temperature drops rapidly. The lack of clouds means that there is no layer of insulation to prevent heat being radiated back into space. Even in the hottest deserts, the nights are extremely chilly, and the temperature may drop to the freezing point.

The fall in temperature during the hours of darkness does, however, bring some benefit.

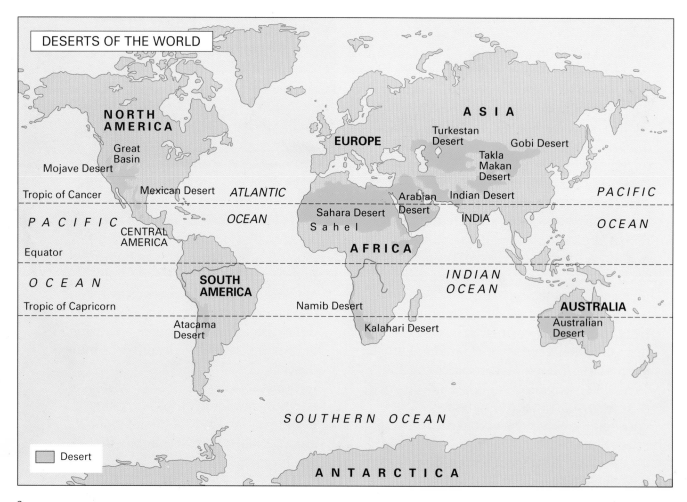

DESERTS OF THE WORLD

NORTH AMERICA
Great Basin
Mojave Desert
Tropic of Cancer
Mexican Desert
ATLANTIC
PACIFIC
OCEAN
CENTRAL AMERICA
Equator
OCEAN
Tropic of Capricorn
SOUTH AMERICA
Atacama Desert

EUROPE
Sahara Desert
Sahel
AFRICA
Namib Desert
Kalahari Desert

ASIA
Turkestan Desert
Gobi Desert
Takla Makan Desert
Arabian Desert
Indian Desert
INDIA
PACIFIC
OCEAN

INDIAN OCEAN
AUSTRALIA
Australian Desert

SOUTHERN OCEAN

Desert

ANTARCTICA

△ Some deserts in China are dry and cold.

Sometimes the temperature falls low enough to cause some of the water vapor in the air to be deposited as dew by **condensation**. This small amount of water is vital to some forms of desert life.

Desert formation

There are three main reasons for the lack of rain that leads to the formation of deserts:

Equatorial wind belts.   Around the equator, which receives the full effect of sunlight throughout the year, warm air is constantly rising. This creates wind belts that blow north and south away from the equator. As the air rises, it cools and loses nearly all of its water as rain. When the air descends back to the earth's surface around the Tropics of Capricorn and Cancer, it is too dry for clouds to form. Without clouds, no rain can fall, and so a desert forms. Most of the world's deserts are a result of these equatorial wind belts, including the Sahara, Kalahari, Arabian, Indian, Australian, and Mexican deserts.

Rain shadows.   Some parts of the earth's land surface, in the middle of the great continents, are too far from the sea for rain-bearing winds to reach them. Any moisture that is in the air falls as it passes over high mountain ranges, and land that lies beyond the mountains receives little or no rain. In some places this has created cool, high-altitude deserts. The Great Basin in the United States, and the Takla Makan and Gobi deserts in China, have formed in the rain shadow of mountains. Although they are deserts, these regions are cold and often covered with snow during the winter.

Cold currents.   The southwestern coasts of Africa and South America are swept by cold currents welling up from the ocean bottom. The currents cool the air that passes over them, causing the water in the air to fall as rain before it reaches the land. The Namib and Atacama deserts have formed as a result of these cold currents. The only water that regularly reaches these coastal deserts comes in the form of early morning sea fogs.

Desert landscapes

The land in deserts is almost completely bare of vegetation, and in many cases it is bare of soil as well. An important basic feature of deserts is that there is not enough water to sustain a mat of vegetation to protect the soil and hold it together. The soils are exposed to the full effects of the harsh climate, so they break down quickly and are blown away by the wind. Alternate heating and cooling causes rocks to fracture into stones, rock flakes, and smaller particles, which can also be blown about. The effects of strong sunlight can change some soils chemically, giving them a characteristic red color. Rainstorms can destroy the land surface: Storm water rushing down hillsides can cut steep gullies and wash away tons of soil.

The long-term effects of climate and erosion have produced four main desert landscapes. Most deserts consist of a mixture of all four landscapes. Contrary to the popular image, deserts are not full of sand dunes and nothing else. In fact, sand covers less than 20 percent of the world's desert areas.

Stony deserts are bare plains covered with stones and gravel, with occasional areas of flat, bare rock. Most stony deserts also contain ranges of steep-sided hills.

Claypan deserts are large areas covered with mud and clay that have been baked hard by the sun. Salt flats are the dried remains of saltwater seas and lakes. These are the most inhospitable areas, as few plants and animals can tolerate the very salty conditions.

In sandy deserts such as the Sahara, Arabian, and Turkestan deserts, thousands of square miles of the earth's surface are covered with sand that is constantly in motion. Series of dunes march across the desert like slow-motion waves, moving at 65 feet per year. The largest of these dunes reach 1,000 feet high. They are found in the heart of the desert, where the shifting sand threatens to smother everything.

Desert fringes

Around the hotter edges of many deserts are areas of semidesert which have a higher annual rainfall, but are still very dry environments. These desert fringes are the areas that attract the largest number of human inhabitants. In Africa and Asia, these people are usually **nomads** who drive herds of livestock, traveling in search of areas where rain has fallen recently and the land is green. As they travel, the nomads use large amounts of the dried-up vegetation for fuel.

▷ Nomads traveling by camel in Algeria

▽ A stony landscape in the Sahara

9

△ Many desert trees lose their leaves in summer and appear to be dead. But the trunk and branches can withstand the sun, and new leaves come out when the season gets cooler.

◁ An oasis in Morocco, on the northern edge of the Sahara Desert

Water in the desert

Deserts are not completely dry, although there is little water visible on the surface. Nearly all the water is underground, but some natural springs and water holes are found throughout most desert areas. These vary in size from small trickles that yield a few gallons of water a day, to lakes containing millions of gallons. Around all but the smallest water holes an oasis of lush green vegetation usually marks the presence of water. The largest oases supply water to fields which can feed several thousand people.

There are also rivers in the desert. For most of the year these watercourses, which are known by the Arabic name wadi, have no running water. However, there is often underground water just below the dry wadi bed. Some vegetation grows all year along many wadis, and fields are sometimes planted. But a sudden rainstorm can fill the wadi with floodwater, washing away all but the most firmly rooted plants.

Survival strategies

Desert plants and animals can survive the hostile conditions because they have become adapted to their environment. Nearly all desert adaptations are part of survival strategies that are directed toward two vital goals: obtaining enough water, and maintaining the correct body temperature.

The water balance

Plant and animal tissues consist mainly of water. If more than a certain amount of that water is lost, then the plant or animal dies. In general, desert species can tolerate the loss of more water than species that live in other parts of the world. This ability to make do with very little water is the most common of all desert adaptations.

Desert plants tend to have long and elaborate root systems, and often have a waxy coating to prevent water being lost to the atmosphere. Some plants can store large amounts of water in their tissue after a

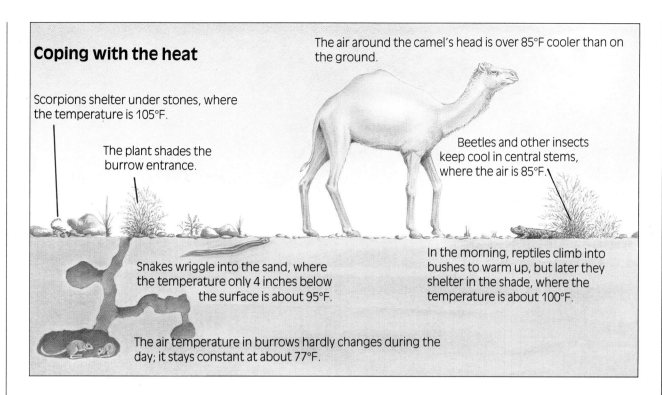

Coping with the heat

The air around the camel's head is over 85°F cooler than on the ground.

Scorpions shelter under stones, where the temperature is 105°F.

The plant shades the burrow entrance.

Beetles and other insects keep cool in central stems, where the air is 85°F.

In the morning, reptiles climb into bushes to warm up, but later they shelter in the shade, where the temperature is about 100°F.

Snakes wriggle into the sand, where the temperature only 4 inches below the surface is about 95°F.

The air temperature in burrows hardly changes during the day; it stays constant at about 77°F.

rainstorm, and the stored water enables them to survive a drought. Some desert animals, such as the camel, can also survive long periods between drinking. Other animals get all the water they need from vegetation, even from dry seeds. Predators tend to get most of the water they need from the blood and other body fluids of their prey. Most desert animals conserve water by producing very dry dung. Many reptiles take this a stage further by passing solid crystals rather than liquid urine.

Keeping cool

Water is doubly precious in the desert because it is extremely useful for cooling. As water evaporates, it removes heat from the surface it is lying on. Some animals, such as humans, cool themselves by sweating. Others, such as dogs, cool themselves by panting and letting their saliva evaporate from their tongues. Desert species have reduced these functions to a minimum. In an emergency, some cool themselves by spraying their feet with urine.

Another strategy for avoiding the heat of the day is to operate only at night. Many desert animals are nocturnal and spend the daylight hours in deep shade or below the ground. Animals that are active during the day have developed methods for avoiding

the heat of the sun and for reducing contact with the hot ground to a minimum.

Some desert plants and animals avoid the summer months completely by entering a state of almost complete inactivity, called dormancy. A few small desert mammals enter a state of summer hibernation known as aestivation. Sealed within a burrow, the animal can sleep through the summer, living off reserves of fat.

Finding food

In deserts, plants and animals exist in much smaller numbers than elsewhere, and are much more widely spaced from each other. It has been estimated that in the Sahara Desert, there is about one mouse for every two square miles.

The extreme conditions in the desert make the struggle for food especially critical. For predators, it is vital that every attack has the dead certainty of a quick kill. Many desert animals produce powerful venoms.

condensation—process by which water vapor in the atmosphere turns back into a liquid.
nomads—people who have no permanent settlements.

Plants in the sand

Plants bring life to the desert. Without them, there would be no animal life. But unlike animals, plants cannot move to avoid the sun. Rooted in place, desert plants have adapted in several different ways in order to endure the heat and drought. Despite the barren appearance of deserts, they contain many more plants than you might think.

Fast flowers

The most numerous plants in the desert are annuals, plants that grow from seed each year. These plants have no drought-resistant qualities. They survive in the desert by spending very little time as growing plants—most of the year they are dormant seeds. These desert plants are known as **ephemerals** because they grow for such a short time. Some of them retain their seeds in pods on top of withered stems, but many others scatter their seeds at the end of their short growing season. Countless millions of seeds are produced each year to be blown by the wind, baked by the sun, and buried in the top layers of soil. The seeds may lie dormant for up to three years, almost completely dry and apparently lifeless. Many small desert animals feed on these seeds, and a great many are eaten each year. However, so many seeds are produced that

▽ The Mojave Desert comes to life after rain (inset). Late summer flowers in the Namib Desert (below) are a great tourist attraction.

△ Sand builds up around the roots of grasses.

Mojave Desert can be as colorful as an alpine meadow, a riot of bright California poppies, clover, and goldfields. But within a few weeks, the ephemeral plants will complete their brief annual lives, and the desert again takes on a burned, brown appearance.

Holding firm

Another group of desert plants that are often overlooked are the perennial grasses. Unlike annual plants, perennials do not grow from seed each year. Instead, they reproduce by growing new shoots from their root systems. Over the years, these root systems become large and complex, with as much as 85 percent of a plant growing underground. The extensive root system enables the plant to collect water from a wide area. During the driest months, the root system stays alive below the surface, while above ground the vegetation appears to shrivel and die.

Such plants are especially important in areas of sandy desert because they help to hold together the shifting desert surface. Many of them can produce roots from any part that becomes buried by sand. As a result, it is hard for them to become completely smothered—they just take root again and grow their way back into the sunlight. Sand and soil blown by the wind gradually build up around the plant and become bound together by the tangled root system. Small mounds, up to 10 feet across, can form around such plants, and are a familiar sight in desert areas. These mounds create shelter and a fairly stable environment for other forms of desert life.

In the more sheltered parts of a sandy desert, plants such as three awl grass may even take hold of the very crest of a dune. For a short while the plant may succeed in holding this high ground, but eventually it will become lost in the shifting sand. In other ecosystems, the first plants to take root in bare ground are known as pioneer species because they will be gradually replaced by other plants until the vegetation reaches a **climax community**. In the desert, however, conditions are so harsh that in most cases pioneer species are the climax community.

some are bound to survive until the next time it rains.

As soon as the rain has soaked into the soil, the seeds begin to germinate. Some plants grow very quickly indeed. Shoots appear overnight, and within days the desert is carpeted with tiny flowers. When fully grown, these plants consist of no more than a short stalk and a flower which appears to be growing straight out of the bare ground. For these plants, often found in the drier desert areas, life is a race against time to flower and produce seeds before becoming shriveled by the sun. Other ephemeral plants grow taller and therefore need more moisture than a single rainstorm. These plants delay germination until the second or third rainfall, by means of an outer coating on the seeds that gradually washes off.

In places where the scant annual rainfall arrives on a regular basis, for example in the Mojave Desert in the United States, a wide variety of flowering plants have become established. In April, Antelope Valley in the

True desert plants

The ephemeral flowers and perennial grasses are widespread in deserts, but they are not true desert plants. They both belong to groups of plants that grow best in cooler, wetter conditions. The desert members of these groups are those plants that were best able to adapt to conditions of permanent drought. True desert plants often have much more extreme adaptations, and include some of the oddest plants on earth.

Water storage

One solution to the problem of living in dry areas is for a plant to absorb plenty of water when it is available and then store it in special tissue, known as succulent tissue. Plants that store water in this way are often called succulents. The most well known succulents are the cacti. The cacti, more than 2,000 species of them, are native only to North and South America, although some species have been introduced to other parts of the world and now grow wild.

Cacti can take in and store large quantities of water. They tend to have shallow root systems that extend over a wide area. After a rainstorm, a large cactus can take in as much as a ton of water, expanding in size until it has a tight and swollen appearance. During the months in between rainstorms, the cactus will gradually shrink as the stored

△ Hedgehog cactus

◁ Fishhook barrel cactus

The fight to save water

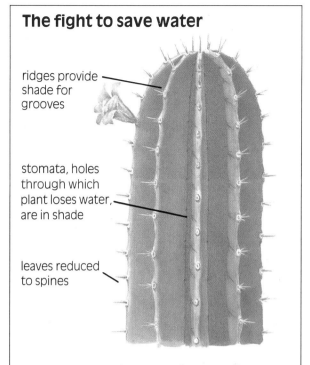

ridges provide shade for grooves

stomata, holes through which plant loses water, are in shade

leaves reduced to spines

Spines play a role in preventing water loss. They help to break up air currents, forming a thin layer of still air round the plant. Evaporation is slower in still air than in moving air.

water is used up, until its outer surface is seamed and lined.

A prickly tale

The prickly pear has two features that make it attractive to humans: It produces a fruit that can be eaten (with difficulty, hence the name) and it can be grown in hedges to enclose livestock. Soon after its discovery, the prickly pear was brought back to Europe, and it is now found in many places around the Mediterranean Sea. The trouble began when human settlers took the prickly pear to Australia. They thought that the cactus would prove invaluable for dividing up Australia's dry grasslands.

They were almost right. The cactus proved very successful. Coming from a distant continent, the prickly pear had no natural enemies or competitors in Australia. It thrived in its new environment, and soon thousands of square miles were covered by prickly pears and nothing else. The prickly pear, a harmless desert plant in America, is now considered a serious threat to farmland in Australia.

Cowboy cactus

The most well known desert plant, by shape if not by name, is the saguaro cactus, which is found in northern Mexico and the southwestern United States. This is the cactus that is familiar from a thousand cowboy films.

Despite being covered with a host of spines, and being deadly poisonous, the saguaro is a remarkably hospitable plant. The shade and cool surfaces it provides are used by a variety of small animals, and many insects live on the cactus itself. Near the top of the plant, desert woodpeckers may create nest holes, which in following years may be occupied by other birds such as desert owls.

Sadly, the saguaro has now joined the list of endangered plants. These huge cacti, up to 50 feet high, are literally disappearing from the desert overnight. In the drier parts of the United States, it has become fashionable in recent years to have one or two saguaro cacti in the garden. A full-grown cactus might be worth thousands of dollars. Like all cacti, the saguaro is very slow growing. The only way that garden suppliers could meet demand was by taking wild cacti from the desert. The problem has become so serious that several states now employ armed cactus rangers to protect the endangered saguaros. Nighttime gunfights between the rangers and cactus thieves have become fairly commonplace.

◁ △ Woodpeckers (left) and owls (top) nest in the saguaro cactus (above).

△ The mallee adds a splash of color to the Australian Desert.

Woody survivors

The other important group of desert plants are the shrubs and stunted trees. These are found mostly in stony deserts, but they occur in all desert areas. The southern reaches of the Sahara Desert are dominated by many drought-resistant species of acacia, many of them extremely thorny. Some thornbushes form mounds in the same way as some of the perennial grasses. These thornbush mounds can reach over 32 feet in diameter. In the sun-baked mountains of the central Sahara, dwarf cypresses grow in the shade of narrow, steep-sided gullies.

Acacias are also found in many parts of the Australian Desert, but in some districts their place is taken by mallees, which are related to the eucalyptus. Much of the central Asian deserts are occupied by the shrublike saxaul trees. In the American deserts, the creosote bush (so called because it smells like the wood preservative creosote) is one of the most widespread desert plants. These desert shrubs and trees usually have extremely long root systems, with individual roots stretching up to 250 feet. These long roots bring water from deep underground and anchor the plant firmly in the shifting desert, particularly if they get a hold on solid rock.

Many of these shrubs lose their leaves in summer, and some even shed most of their branches as well. Without leaves, the plant's internal workings slow down and almost come to a standstill. During the hottest part of the year, the plant remains in a dormant condition. The tough woody tissues of the trunk and main branches are very resistant to the effects of the sun, and some shrubs can dry out almost completely without dying. When the weather turns slightly cooler, and the rains begin to fall, new leaves and shoots start to grow on apparently dead branches. One result of this stop-start life cycle is that the plants grow extremely slowly and live to a great age by human standards. Some of the pine trees in the California deserts are more than 2,000 years old.

These pine trees are, however, mere youngsters compared with some creosote bushes. These bushes survive desert conditions by having a very extensive root system which absorbs every drop of moisture from the surface layer of soil. As a result, no other plant can live nearby, and creosote bushes are usually surrounded by a circle of bare ground. A few bushes that have very efficient root systems have managed to grow undisturbed for thousands of years. During this time, the bush has gradually formed a hollow ring as the older stems in the middle die off. The largest bushes now measure more than 80 feet across. Although the visible branches may only be a few centuries old, a creosote bush of that size has been living for at least 10,000 years.

Many of the plants found in deserts are members of plant groups that are found all over the world. But in some cases, the natural vegetation of a desert represents a very special solution to a very special set of conditions.

The inland part of Chile's Atacama Desert is too high above sea level to gain any benefit from sea fogs. Almost the only moisture to reach this dry plateau comes in the form of great floods that wash down from the Andes about once every 10 years. Maps prepared by the first European explorers show that large parts of this desert were once covered by dense jungles of tamarugo trees. The tamarugo is unique to this part of Chile, and has the astonishing ability to

withstand the 10-year droughts between floods. Unfortunately, the explorers who discovered these jungles were soon followed by settlers who began cutting down the tamarugo trees for firewood.

All this happened hundreds of years ago, and today only a few isolated areas of tamarugos are left. Chilean scientists are currently studying how to set about reintroducing the tamarugo on a large scale. As well as preventing soil erosion from the 10-yearly floods, the trees would also provide considerable quantities of fruit that could be used as animal food.

Fog-loving leaves

The Namib Desert, on the west coast of southern Africa, is home to one of the world's strangest plants. Welwitschia has a huge swollen root up to three feet across, the upper part of which projects above the surface of the ground. From the top of this swollen root sprout the plant's leaves. These trail from welwitschia like coiled straps, and never stop growing. Under perfect conditions, the leaves would grow hundreds of feet long during the plant's 100-year life span. However, the harsh conditions of the desert mean that the leaves are continually being worn and frayed and rarely reach more than a few feet in the wild. Welwitschia needs a lot of leaf area because it uses its leaves to absorb the moisture and condensation produced by sea fogs. Inside the leaves, a network of fine tubes carries the precious water to the swollen root where it is stored.

◁ The creosote bush has a distinctive smell which gives it its name.

▷ The welwitschia absorbs moisture from the sea fogs that reach the Namib Desert.

ephemerals—desert plants that grow for only a short time after it has rained.
climax community—the final, stable form of the natural vegetation within any ecosystem.

From insects to reptiles

The most numerous animals in the desert, as in other land ecosystems, are the insects. Most of the major groups of insects—flies, cockroaches, beetles, butterflies, grasshoppers, ants, wasps, and bees—contain many desert-dwelling species. Those insects that live in water during the early part of their lives, such as dragonflies and mosquitoes, are not widely found in deserts because there is very little open water.

Design for survival

Insect body design is well suited to desert conditions. The hard outer covering, or cuticle, that surrounds an insect's body is composed of a tough waterproof substance known as chitin. As a result, insects lose very little moisture by evaporation.

All animals lose water while breathing. When insects exhale, they breathe out water vapor as well as carbon dioxide through holes on the body called spiracles. They do not breathe continuously. They use special muscles to keep their spiracles closed until the amount of carbon dioxide in their bodies reaches a certain level. Only then do they open their spiracles and exhale, so water loss is kept to a minimum. Some desert insects can actually absorb water vapor through the lower part of their abdomens.

Like other desert animals, many insects do not drink at all. They get the small amounts of water they need from their food, which means that they can survive long periods of drought. Some desert insects, however, do need to drink and have developed some unusual ways of doing so. One beetle from the Namib Desert kneels to drink the morning fog. The insect positions itself with its head near the ground and its abdomen sticking up into the air. When the

△ Long legs keep the beetle's body away from the burning sand. All the world's longest-legged beetles are desert species. One beetle stands on its head (inset) to drink fog moisture from its body.

fog rolls in from the sea, water droplets condense on the beetle's abdomen and run down its body into its mouth.

Insect activity in the desert is at its highest shortly after it has rained. Insects of all types exploit the short-lived abundance of ephemeral plants and many insects breed and lay eggs at this time. The eggs of some species hatch almost immediately so that the larvae can also take advantage of the greenery. Some of these will then spend the months of drought in a dormant state as a pupa. In other species, the eggs remain dormant during the dry period and hatch with the next rains. The large number of eggs and pupae produced each year form a valuable food resource for other animals, especially lizards. But as with ephemeral plant seeds, enough survive to ensure the next generation.

Pots of honey

Several species of desert ants have developed a unique method of surviving the long periods of drought. These ants are often known as honey-pot ants. After it has rained, the ants can collect far more nectar from ephemeral plants than they can eat. A number of individuals in the ant colony are designated as storage vessels. These ants, which are known as repletes, attach themselves to the roof of the ant colony. The rest of the ants then feed the repletes with nectar until their bodies swell to the size of grapes. The repletes remain in this condition for up to 10 months, gradually shrinking as they feed the colony during the drought.

The repletes also represent an attractive food source for other animals, including human beings. To some of the people who live on the fringes of deserts, the discovery of a honey-pot ant colony means a delicious feast.

▽ Honey-pot ant

Keeping cool

Many insects avoid the worst of the desert's heat by spending as much time as possible below the surface in the top layer of soil or sand. Some build permanent burrows and emerge at certain times to feed, while others can just "swim" into the loosely packed desert surface at the first sign of danger.

Most winged insects fly about at night. There are two main reasons for this. First, the lower temperatures at night mean that there is less danger of the insect over-heating. The muscle activity involved in flying generates a lot of heat in an insect's body. During the sunlit hours, when the air temperature is fairly high, insects cannot lose heat quickly enough to fly any distance. The second reason is that flying is easier at night. By day, desert air is too dry and thin to provide much resistance to the wings of an insect, so much of the muscle power is wasted. When the air cools at night, it becomes damper and denser, and an insect's wings work more efficiently.

A plague from the desert

The desert is home to the most fearsome of all insect pests, the desert locust. Locusts are related to the humble grasshopper, but unlike their relatives, they gather in huge swarms which can travel thousands of miles in search of food. A large swarm may cover 400 square miles, and may contain up to 40 billion locusts. When a swarm of this size lands, it can cause enormous damage, eating up to 40,000 tons of vegetation every day. In human terms, that represents enough food to supply a city of 400,000 inhabitants for a whole year. The locust problem is made more complicated by the fact that the appearance of a swarm is completely unpredictable.

The locust breeding season is timed to coincide with the rains, because female locusts can only lay their eggs in damp ground. In some species, the eggs can remain dormant underground for up to three years, but most hatch within three to four weeks. The young locusts cannot fly and are known as hoppers. The hoppers form into bands of up to 20,000 insects, and march off in search of food. At night the hoppers often roost in trees, and use the morning sunlight to warm their bodies before they set off on the day's march. Hoppers eat voraciously as they grow, and by the time they get their wings, they have usually eaten all the vegetation within easy reach. The locusts then take to the sky in search of food, gathering into huge swarms for journeys that may cover 3,000 miles.

The desert locust is one of the very few aspects of desert ecology that threatens humans, because crops and fields are especially vulnerable to the swarms. Wherever possible, locusts are exterminated at every point in their life cycle—as eggs, as hoppers, and as adults; and every conceivable weapon is used against them—insecticides, fire, explosives, and even poison gas.

As many as 1,000 locusts may lay their eggs (top left) on the same square yard of ground. When the young locusts, called hoppers, hatch they cannot fly (center left), but they soon develop wing buds (bottom left). Adult locusts (above) fly in huge swarms.

△ A wolf spider with its egg sac

▽ A trap-door spider with the door of its hole

Spiders and scorpions

Spiders are found in all parts of the desert, their number depending on the size of the insect populations on which they prey. Few desert spiders spin webs to catch flying insects. Most take their prey on the ground. In Australia and North America, tarantulas and trap-door spiders are the main species, but these species are not very numerous in the Sahara, where wolf spiders and jumping spiders are among the most widespread.

Most desert spiders live in underground burrows, and have sturdy bodies typical of digging animals. Those that live on the surface tend to be smaller and lighter.

Heat resistant

Scorpions are probably the hardiest of all desert creatures. They can survive higher temperatures than either insects or spiders and have the lowest water-loss rate of any desert animal. Despite their fearsome reputation, scorpions are timid and solitary creatures, ranging from small black scorpions of about ¾ inch to large yellow scorpions measuring 5 inches long.

Desert scorpions are almost completely nocturnal. Many spend the day in burrows that may be a yard in length and reach 30 inches below the surface. Other species bury themselves in shallow scrapes in loose soil or shelter beneath rocks and vegetation. At night they emerge to feed. Scorpions hunt by wandering slowly over the desert surface, sensing their prey mainly with fine hairs on the front of their heads. When a scorpion encounters a large insect, a spider, or even another scorpion, it immediately seizes its prey in its pincers and the tail rises to deliver the killing sting. Some scorpion venom is among the most deadly of all animal poisons and is

capable of killing a human within a few hours and a dog within a few minutes.

Camel spiders

Perhaps the most perfectly adapted of all desert animals are the camel spiders. They are not true spiders; they belong to their own separate group and are related to both spiders and scorpions. In some places they are also known as wind scorpions. They look like large, hairy spiders, measuring about 5 inches across. Camel spiders are only found in deserts, and then only in the most barren parts. They avoid areas of activity such as oases, preferring the open spaces of the empty desert. Most of the time they remain unseen in burrows. When hungry, they emerge at night as fierce predators.

Camel spiders locate their prey, such as scorpions, lizards, mice, and small birds, by running at random across the desert. On their long legs, camel spiders can run almost too fast for the human eye to follow. Any suitable animal that they encounter is soon chased, caught, and eaten. Camel spiders will carry on eating until their bodies are swollen with food, and they can barely crawl back to their burrows. By reducing the amount of time they spend on the surface to an absolute minimum, camel spiders greatly increase their own chances of survival.

△ A giant desert scorpion poised to attack

△ This lizard, the horned toad, turns paler during the day to reflect the heat.

Cold blood in hot deserts

Reptiles are the most numerous of desert **vertebrates,** both in number of species and in the size of the overall populations. Desert reptiles range from an inch to over 5 feet in length, and they are found in all parts of the desert ecosystem. Almost all of them are carnivores, that is, they hunt and eat other animals. Most of the smaller lizards feed on insects, although some also eat certain types of vegetation. The larger desert reptiles mainly hunt other vertebrates—lizards, small mammals, and birds.

Reptiles are cold-blooded. Unlike mammals and birds, they do not generate their own body heat. Reptiles are much more dependent on their environment: They must obtain the heat energy needed to operate their bodies from the sun.

Toad tactics

The importance of sunlight to desert reptiles is neatly illustrated by the horned toad, which is actually a species of lizard found in the North American deserts. This small reptile has an unusual adaptation that gives it a small early morning advantage over the other reptiles with which it competes for food.

When it wakes just before dawn, the horned toad is slow and sluggish. It crawls from its burrow and positions itself so that it receives the first rays of the sun. As sunlight falls on the horned toad, the animal warms up, helped by the fact that its dark colors absorb heat better than light ones. As the morning gets hotter, the reptile gradually gets lighter in color. Light colors reflect heat better than dark ones and this enables the horned toad to stay in the sun longer.

There is no overall advantage in being either pale or dark in the desert as far as heat is concerned; the advantages cancel each other out. But by changing color as the day progresses, the horned toad extracts a double advantage.

Shadow and light

Although reptiles can take full advantage of the sun, they are at its mercy when it comes to keeping cool. Their main method of keeping cool is to avoid the sun, which many desert reptiles do by shadow hopping.

This important aspect of desert reptile behavior consists of alternating short dashes across open ground with longer rests in the shade of rocks or vegetation. As the heat of the day increases, the periods spent in sunlight get shorter and the time spent in the shade increases, until the animal eventually retreats to its burrow. By shadow hopping like this, some desert lizards can maintain a near-constant body temperature for up to five hours of surface activity.

Desert monster

The largest of the desert reptiles is the desert monitor, which is found throughout the Sahara, Arabian, Indian, and central Asian deserts. A full grown adult may measure up to 5 feet in length, and can run at speeds of up to 6 mph over short distances, which is a considerable achievement for such a large reptile. Desert monitors lead a solitary existence, and follow a set daily routine. Each morning the monitor sets off in search of food. This daily walk usually follows exactly the same route, past any likely places where small mammals, birds, and lizards may nest. In areas where food is especially scarce, the daily "shopping expedition" may mean a walk of up to three miles. When the desert monitor locates its prey, perhaps a rodent sleeping in its burrow, it is strong enough to dig down and seize its prey before it can escape. If the prey does manage to escape, the monitor is well equipped to give chase.

Surefooted?

Heat is not the only problem for animal life in the desert. Some parts of the desert environment present special problems to animal movement. The shifting sands of the dunes are especially hazardous. A single misplaced step can send the animal tumbling into danger. Two groups of small reptiles that are found throughout the deserts, the geckos and the skinks, have adapted to meet this problem in two very different ways.

Many desert geckos have fringes of hairs around their feet and toes. These fringes prevent the animals' feet from sinking into the sand, and enable them to scamper with great agility in search of insect prey. One species of gecko, which lives in the extremely dry Namib Desert, has webbed feet even though it will never walk on damp ground, let alone swim. The webs of skin between the toes have the same function as the fringes of hair on its relatives—they enable the gecko to take certain steps in an uncertain environment.

Skinks take a different approach to dry sand. Their legs have become shorter and their bodies more rounded. One species has even lost its legs completely. These skinks travel by swimming through the sand like fish. Although they often hunt insects on the surface, they can wriggle beneath the sand and disappear at the first sign of danger.

Shifting sideways

The desert also has its fair share of snakes, although, like other predators, their numbers are fairly small. Some come out at night to hunt lizards and small mammals. Others lie in ambush during the day, buried in sand with only their heads above the surface. One of the best adapted of all desert snakes is the

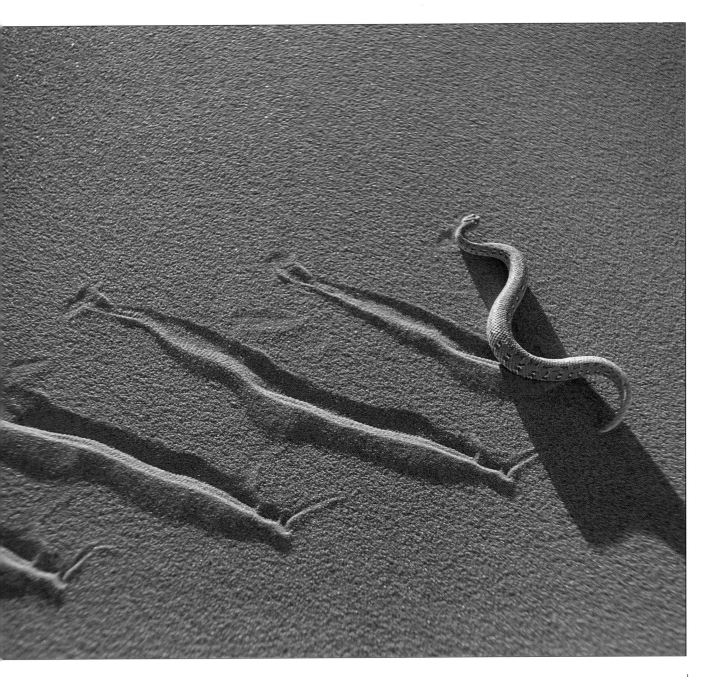

△ The tracks of the sidewinder snake are easy to identify.

◁ The web-footed gecko does not sink into the sand.

sidewinder of the North American deserts. As its name suggests, the sidewinder has an unusual method of movement that is ideally suited to sandy desert conditions.

Most other snakes pull themselves forward along the ground, using their flexible rib cage almost like a series of internal legs. On loose sand, this method is less efficient than on hard-packed earth. The sidewinder pulls itself sideways instead. The snake makes a series of loops in the

direction it wants to travel, and then pulls the rest of its body to follow. This method enables the animal to use its body as a lever, which is a great advantage on loose sand. The sidewinder is a very effective nocturnal hunter, and its characteristic track of disconnected S shapes is most often seen in the early morning light.

reptiles—cold-blooded vertebrates (see below) with scaly bodies.
vertebrates—animals that have backbones and internal skeletons.

27

Mammals and birds

Rodents and other mammals

Mammals are warm-blooded animals that generate heat inside their own bodies. They maintain a steady body temperature that is completely independent of environmental conditions and have developed ways of preventing overheating when very active. So it is not surprising that a fairly large number of mammals have adapted to the hot, dry conditions of the desert. In general, lack of food in the desert is a greater problem for mammals than the lack of water.

Small mammals, particularly plant-eating **rodents**, are the most widespread and numerous of desert mammals. In the deserts of Africa and Asia, gerbils and girds are the main species, closely followed by jerboas and some mice. In North America, desert gophers and kangaroo rats occupy similar positions in the desert food chains.

Air conditioning

Small desert mammals are almost completely nocturnal. They spend the day safe in their burrows beneath the desert floor. Many mammals seal the entrances to their burrows each time they enter and leave it. This not only conceals the entrance from predators, it also helps keep conditions in the burrow more comfortable.

Whatever the temperature at the surface, there is a layer about three feet below the surface where the temperature remains fairly constant. This is the level at which most of the small mammal burrows are to be found. Some species prefer to dig deeper, up to 10 feet below the surface, while others make shallower burrows, particularly during cool winter months.

As well as providing an environment with a constant and acceptable temperature, a sealed burrow also helps conserve water. As the mammal exhales, water vapor in its breath is absorbed by the dry air trapped inside the burrow. Gradually the amount of water in the air builds up until the humidity is quite high. Under these conditions of increased humidity, the mammal loses much less water by evaporation.

Keeping cool below ground

The bars on this graph show typical summer temperatures of the air and sand in a hot desert. Notice that the temperature in the burrow stays fairly even day and night.

▽ Kangaroo rats, which live in North American deserts, feed on plant seeds.

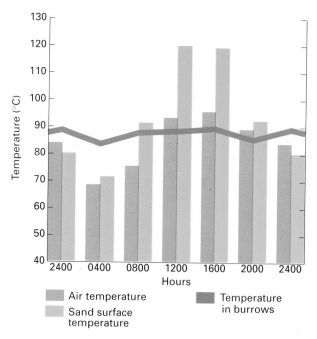

△ Jerboas can run very fast on their two hind legs.

No drinking

Many of the small desert mammals do not require fresh water; they get all the water they need from their food. The most numerous of the desert rodents are those that feed mainly on seeds. At night, the desert comes alive with gerbils, girds, and kangaroo rats all scampering and searching through the surface layers looking for food. Although the seeds may have been buried for months, they still contain a small amount of moisture. The seeds also contain significant amounts of carbohydrates and fats which the animal can convert inside its body to produce some additional water. In an emergency, for example when the drought is especially prolonged, some desert rodents can obtain water from their own stored reserves of fat.

Night racers

Perhaps the most characteristic of all desert mammals are the jerboas. Jerboas are the fastest of all small mammals and can run at speeds up to 22 mph. Their elongated hind legs are the main reason for the jerboas' success. Nighttime activity proceeds in a dizzying series of high-speed runs interspersed with jumps of up to 10 feet. This furious rate of activity means that the jerboa can escape from most of its predators most of the time. If the jerboa tried to be active by day, it would be a different story. Within minutes, the combination of desert sun and physical effort would have raised the animal's temperature and it would collapse with heat exhaustion. Only in the cool of the night is it safe for the jerboa to race about the desert.

The jackrabbit (above) and fennec fox (left) have large ears to keep them cool in the hot deserts where they live.

Familiar wildlife

Hedgehogs and foxes are generally thought of as inhabiting more temperate parts of the world, but they have also adapted well to the desert environment. The desert species of both animals are distinguished by having unusually large ears.

The fennec fox, which inhabits the sandy wastes of the Sahara, hunts mainly at night. During the day, the fennec stays secure in its burrow, which may stretch up to 100 feet into a dune. Like many other nocturnal hunters, the fennec relies largely on its sense of hearing to find its prey, which include rodents and lizards. Its large ears are very good at gathering sound waves and enable it to fix the position of its prey from some distance away.

When the fennec goes out by day, its large ears serve a different purpose, that of keeping cool. Body heat is carried away from the center of the animal by the bloodstream which flows through a network of fine vessels in the ears. Large ears mean a large surface area to radiate away unwanted heat.

Hidden hunter

One of the most unusual of desert mammals is the little-known golden mole from the Namib Desert of southern Africa. Although golden moles closely resemble the black moles found in temperate regions, they are not closely related, and belong to their own separate animal group. Golden moles are completely adapted to life beneath the sand dunes. They have no visible eyes or ears, although their sense of hearing is actually extremely good. Their leg bones have become withdrawn into their bodies, and only their feet stick out. Despite this, they are very good tunnelers and can also "swim" through loose, dry sand.

The golden mole is classified as an insectivore (insect eater), but it also feeds on lizards, especially skinks. One of the skinks found in the Namib Desert has adapted to the sandy conditions so much that it has lost its legs entirely. The legless skink resembles a small, thick eel about 2½ inches long, and spends virtually its whole life beneath the surface.

Desert birds

Birds have a number of built-in advantages over mammals when it comes to dealing with desert conditions. Because of the extra heat generated by flying, their bodies are designed to operate at a higher temperature than those of mammals, so they are better able to tolerate desert heat. Surprisingly, feathers are also an advantage. In other parts of the world, the feathers insulate the bird and keep out the cold. In the desert, the insulating properties of the feathers help keep the animal cool.

The birds' greatest advantage is the power of flight, which gives them easy access to any available water. The sand grouse is unique in having water-absorbent feathers on its breast. While its chicks are too young to fly, the parents will fly up to 20 miles each day to soak up water from a pool or spring and then fly back to their nest. The young sand grouse can then quench their thirst by pecking water from their parents' feathers.

△ The roadrunner cannot fly, but it dashes across the desert floor at high speed.

▽ Sand grouse fly to pools to drink and collect water for their chicks, which drink from the parents' breast feathers (inset).

Large mammals

The numbers of larger mammals in the desert are fairly small because of the scarcity of food and water. In fact most of the larger mammals are domesticated animals, especially sheep and goats. These hardy animals can survive on the poor pasture that is the best that the desert can provide. Their thick insulating coat of wool, which makes them doubly valuable to their human owners, is also useful from the animals' point of view. When the sun goes down, the wool keeps the animals warm against the chill of the desert night. During the day, the thick coat protects them against the worst effects of the sun. Although the temperature on the surface of the coat may rise to 160°F, the temperature next to the animals' skin remains at a much more comfortable 105°F.

Camels

The most celebrated of all desert animals is the camel, the legendary "ship of the desert" that can travel across the empty wastes for days without drinking. Although there are still a few two-humped Bactrian camels living wild in the deserts of central Asia, most are now domesticated. In the Sahara and Arabian deserts, the one-humped camel disappeared from the wild many centuries ago. Today, the one-humped camel is a completely domesticated species.

The most important of the camel's adaptations to the desert is the ability to store large amounts of water in its stomach. After drinking its fill, a camel can last 10 times longer than a human being without needing a drink. When food is plentiful, camels also build up large reserves of fat inside their humps. As these reserves are used up, the humps become lose and baggy. The camel is also adapted to the desert in other ways. The feet have only two toes, which are joined by folds of loose skin. These folds help spread the animal's weight and prevent it sinking into soft sand. A camel can also close its nostrils during sandstorms.

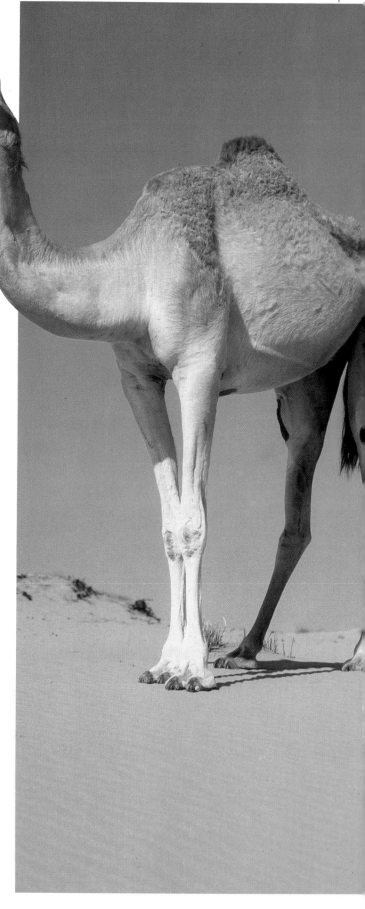

▽ The camel is perhaps the most valuable of all desert animals.

Gazelles

The other large animals commonly found in deserts are various species of antelope and gazelle. Antelope are mainly confined to rocky and mountainous areas. Gazelles prefer gentler landscapes and are even found among sand dunes. During the hottest hours of the day, these animals occupy any available shade, even holes in the ground. When it gets cooler, they wander in search of fresh vegetation, often traveling right through the night. Studies suggest that these animals get all the water they need from vegetation and may spend their whole lives without actually drinking.

Desert gazelles can also allow their body temperature to rise during the day. A special arrangement of blood vessels in the head keep the brain, which is the organ most vulnerable to heat, up to 5.5°F lower than the rest of the body.

▷ A gemsbok oryx in the Namib Desert

Brought back from extinction

Probably the most threatened of all desert wildlife are the addax and oryx antelope. In the Sahara Desert, these animals existed in quite large numbers until about 1900. During this century, thousands of addax and oryx have been slaughtered, especially by soldiers armed with machine guns. Today, there are only a small number remaining, and to catch sight of one is a rare experience.

Further east, in the Arabian Desert, the situation is even worse. By 1972, the Arabian oryx had become completely extinct in the wild. Fortunately, a breeding population had already been established in an American zoo. Some five years later, conservationists were able to start releasing some of the oryx that had been bred in captivity back into the wild.

mammals—warm-blooded vertebrates that feed their young with milk.
rodents—a group of small mammals that have teeth for gnawing.

People and the desert

Most of the desert's human inhabitants are nomads; they have no fixed home, and are forever on the move. Many of the nomads are animal herders and live almost entirely off their flocks and herds. Some nomads also carry out a limited form of agriculture, planting crops when they stop at an oasis and returning to harvest them later in the year.

Primitive peoples

The most primitive peoples to inhabit the desert neither herd animals nor plant crops. They exist on a diet of wild plants and animals and for this reason are known as hunter-gatherers. The men are responsible for hunting and catching meat and may go on long hunting expeditions that can last for days at a time. The women have the less spectacular, but equally important, task of collecting any edible fruits, seeds, and roots that can be found. Their reliance on wild food forces these people to be nomads. The longer they stay in any one place, the harder it becomes to find food.

Only two groups of desert people still follow this way of life: the Aborigines of Australia, and the Bushmen of the Kalahari Desert in southern Africa. Apart from their life-style, these two desert peoples are also interesting for other reasons.

The Aborigines and the Bushmen are the only peoples to have adapted physically to life in the desert.

Aborigines have characteristically broad, flat noses. This feature is believed to have developed in response to the dry, dusty air in the Australian Desert. Many desert mammals also tend to have short, flattened noses. The physical adaptation of the Bushmen is even more noticeable. All human beings have a layer of fat stored beneath our skin. In cool climates this is important for keeping us

△ At least 99.9 percent of the world's population belong to only three racial groups—Caucasian, Negro, and Mongol. The Bushmen of the Kalahari Desert in Africa (above), and the Aborigines of Australia belong to two separate racial groups.

▷ A Bushman mother and her child are using ostrich eggshells as drinking cups.

warm, but in the desert it can be a handicap because the layer of fat prevents the human body from losing heat rapidly. The Bushmen have lost this all-over layer of fat. Their fat stores are concentrated in their buttocks, which leaves the rest of their bodies cooler.

Although we call the Aborigines and Bushmen "primitive" because they have few tools or technology, these peoples live in complete harmony with their harsh environment, and are extremely knowledgeable about it. A thirsty hunter can tell at a glance which particular dried clump of vegetation is attached to a root swollen with lifesaving water. In some respects these primitive peoples know more about desert ecology than most scientists.

Pastoral nomads

Hunter-gatherers are not typical desert inhabitants, and their very basic life-style has been preserved only in the isolated deserts of Australia and southern Africa. Most desert peoples, such as the Bedouin of the Arabian Desert and the Tuareg of the Sahara, are pastoral nomads. Their constant wandering around the desert is dictated by the need to find fresh pasture and grazing for their herds of domesticated animals. Camels, sheep, and goats make up the bulk of these herds, which can outnumber their human owners by 20 to 1.

In general, pastoral nomads meet nearly all their requirements from their flocks and herds. Some of the desert people feed themselves almost entirely on milk provided by their animals, while others boast of eating nothing but meat. Animal hides are put to a variety of uses—they can be stitched together to make tents, water containers, and many other items of equipment and clothing.

Desert caravans

In addition to herding food animals, some desert nomads also have another traditional occupation, that of transporting goods across the desert. Sometimes the goods come from within the desert itself. In the Sahara, for example, blocks of salt are cut from dried salt flats deep in the desert and are carried south to the Sahel.

The camel is the only beast of burden that can withstand desert conditions, and for centuries huge caravans containing hundreds of camels were a major part of the world's trade network. The development of oceangoing ships, and more recently of motor vehicles and airplanes, has led to the virtual disappearance of the camel caravan. Only in the remotest parts of the Sahara and Asian deserts does the camel still have a role as a means of commercial transport.

The success of the camel caravan depended largely on the incredible staying power of the camel. But even camels have to drink sometimes, and the caravan routes

▷ The Tuareg wear robes of many layers to insulate them against the heat. The robes, headdresses, and veils also protect their skin from the harmful effects of strong sunlight.

usually followed the shortest distance between oases and water holes, and some of the oases developed into important trading centers. Where the distance between natural water sources was too great for safety, wells were often dug down to the water beneath the desert surface. Many of these desert wells are still in existence, and some have been in use for hundreds of years.

Waterways beneath the sand

When there is an adequate supply of water, the desert can be extremely fertile. Many oases are surrounded by lush gardens that provide a wide variety of crops for a settled human population.

In the deserts of Iran and Oman, the traditional inhabitants have devised an ingenious method of bringing additional water from the mountains to their desert gardens. The usual method of diverting water to a particular place, in other parts of the world, is to dig a canal. In the desert, however, canals are of little use because of the high rate of evaporation. The Iranian and Omani desert dwellers solve this problem by constructing an underground tunnel, known as a qanat, that may be up to 12 miles in length.

Each qanat begins at a spring in the foothills of the mountains that fringe the deserts. From the spring, the qanat slopes gently downhill until it reaches the garden area, where the water is brought to the surface by means of a well. The qanats are dug entirely by hand by means of a series of vertical shafts that are sunk about every 300

△ Camel caravans are almost a thing of the past, but camels are still used to transport firewood and domestic goods for the desert nomads.

feet or so. Afterward, when the qanat is in use, these shafts provide access for workers who clear any sand that may be clogging up the qanat. Although qanats lie below the desert surface, they are immediately recognizable from the air. The vertical access shafts make a distinctive line of what look like pinpricks in the desert landscape.

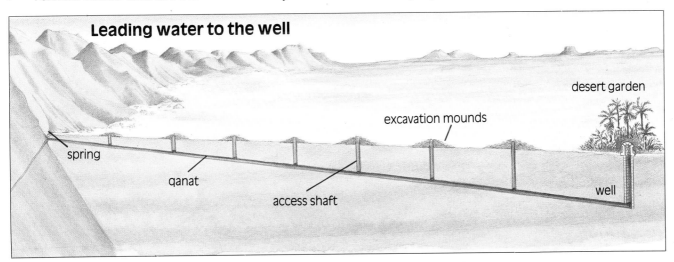

Leading water to the well

spring

qanat

access shaft

excavation mounds

desert garden

well

Fruits of the earth

The crops grown in traditional desert gardens include both cereals and vegetables. Among the most important vegetables are eggplants, tomatoes, onions, peas, carrots, and several varieties of beans. Some gardens also have fruit trees such as oranges, lemons, and figs. However, the single most important plant in the desert gardens is probably the date palm.

Dates, the fruit of the tree, are a valuable food, and many of the desert inhabitants consider dates to be more important than cereals. But as well as being a rich source of food, the date palm also has many other uses. The trunks provide timber to make roof beams and doors for houses and to construct the lifting equipment at wells. Whole palm leaves are used to make temporary huts and fences to enclose livestock, and the ends of the leaves are woven into baskets and sandals. The base of the trunks can be burned as a fuel, and the fibrous tissue that surrounds the trunk can be worked into tough, long-lasting ropes. No part of the tree is wasted, and the tip of the trunk can even be brewed into a strong, sweet wine. Little wonder, then, that the date palm is so highly regarded. It is one of the true treasures of the desert.

▽ Date palm

Goats on the rampage

Goats are quite remarkable beasts. They can tolerate a wide variety of climatic conditions, from cold mountainsides to hot deserts. More importantly, goats can eat almost anything, and can survive on even the poorest quality pasture. These qualities make goats an extremely attractive proposition to the pastoral nomad. However, to the ecologist, goats can often seem to be public enemy number one.

As well as eating small plants down to the ground, and often the roots as well, goats can also attack trees. The agility which enables goats to climb rocky mountainsides also enables them to climb trees to get at the tender green leaves. No vegetation, except large trees—which are rare at the desert fringes—can survive grazing by a herd of goats. Although they are undoubtedly very useful animals if kept under proper control, goats can also be dangerous pests. Many people now consider goats to be little more than "four-legged locusts."

The spreading sand

Desertification is the process by which the ecology of a region changes and it becomes a desert. It is a natural process, which takes place only on the fringes of existing deserts, and is usually linked to changes in the local climate. The Sahara Desert, for example, has been slowly expanding southward for hundreds of years as the climate has got gradually drier.

The presence of large numbers of pastoral nomads greatly accelerates the process of desertification. The flocks and herds of animals consume every scrap of green vegetation, and their human owners then cut down the leafless trees and bushes for firewood. Within a very short time, the land is stripped completely bare, and the nomads have to move on. Behind them they leave an empty landscape that will soon become part of the desert.

The problem is made worse by the fact that the nomads consider their animals to be a sign of wealth, and the more animals the better. They would rather have 40 animals that are dying of starvation than 4 healthy animals that have enough to eat. Slowing down the rate of desertification means educating the nomads to show them how their traditional values might be causing more harm than good.

Soil death

Under natural conditions, the sparse vegetation at the desert fringes forms a delicately balanced ecosystem that is able to withstand all but the most prolonged and severe droughts. When this balance is disturbed, either by overgrazing or by plowing up the land for crops, a series of changes occurs, and the landscape eventually becomes desert. The most important of these changes is that the land loses its most valuable commodity, its soil.

As the natural vegetation is destroyed aboveground, so are the complex root systems below the surface. When the rains do arrive, there are no roots to absorb the water. As a result, the rain washes right through the soil and carries with it the nutrients needed by any surviving plants. Without nutrients, the remaining plants die, and no new plants can grow. The soil dries out and turns to dust, which is then carried away by the wind. Each year around the desert fringes, millions of tons of soil are turned into worthless, windblown dust.

The march of the dunes

A reduction in the number of humans and domesticated animals living in the desert fringes would greatly slow down the process of desertification. But it would not halt the advance of the deserts completely. Stopping the march of the sand dunes requires more human activity, not less.

The desert sand seas are like no other landscape on earth. Driven by the wind, their surface is constantly in motion and, as at sea, the wind creates great waves which we call sand dunes. The commonest of these are the crescent-shaped dunes which are known as barchans. These form where the wind always blows from the same direction, and the horns of the crescent point in the same direction as the wind. Barchans advance because sand is constantly being blown up the long face of the dune and around the sides along the horns. Eventually the horns sweep so far forward that the center of the barchan blows out, the horns form two separate dunes, and the process begins again.

Battling against the sand

Year after year, the desert dunes slowly and steadily advance, smothering everything in their path. Traditional methods of halting the dunes rely on physical barriers. Fences of thornbush are built around fields, and stone walls may even be built around valuable wells. But these barriers can only hold back the sand for a limited time. Eventually so much sand will build up behind them that they are overwhelmed and buried.

▽ Soil erosion in Kenya

◁ Ripples and dunes in the Namib Desert

More recently, efforts have been concentrated on the only permanent method of halting the dunes—covering them with a layer of living vegetation. Long-term stabilization needs larger plants such as drought-resistant shrubs, and these will only take permanent root with a little help from human beings.

In Iran, which has over 12.5 million acres of sand dunes, the government has been spraying the sand dunes with oil in order to give the shrubs a head start. After the dunes have been sprayed, the shrubs are planted in a series of narrow furrows cut across the direction of the wind. The coating of oil on the surface of the dune prevents the seedlings from being blown away, and also helps retain moisture. One area, covering more than 23 square miles, was treated in this manner, and in six years was transformed from bare sand into a thriving forest of trees standing more than 10 feet high.

Desert drivers

In Southern California, desert sand dunes have become a play area for many city dwellers. Each weekend, thousands of people take to the desert with a wide variety of dune buggies and dune bikes. But despite their barren appearance, the dunes are home to many small desert animals that rest in their burrows during the day while the desert drivers are enjoying themselves. Quite apart from the noise and disturbance, there is a serious risk that many mammals and lizards could be crushed to death while they sleep. Even more serious is the fact that seven species of desert plants that grow on the dunes are now in danger of extinction. From the drivers' point of view, the plants are just weeds, and therefore not worth saving anyway. From a desert viewpoint, however, these plants are part of the ecosystem, and their loss could well affect other desert species.

Greening the desert

Turning the desert into useful farmland is an age-old dream. Despite the harsh climate and the widespread destruction of soils, parts of the desert are very fertile—all that is needed is water. Traditionally, small areas have been watered by qanats and wells, but these methods of irrigation are of little use for feeding large numbers of people. Modern desert farmers must use large-scale irrigation if they are to grow enough food for the rapidly increasing population.

If you fly over parts of the Saharan and Arabian deserts, you will notice that the desert is dotted with huge circular wheat fields. From above, the fields stand out as islands of bright green in a sea of pale browns and yellows. These fields, financed by the income from oil production, have enabled countries such as Saudi Arabia to grow all the wheat they need. This is no small achievement for a desert country.

The water used to irrigate these fields comes from deep below the desert and is brought to the surface by motorized pumps. The circular shape of the fields is created by the way the ground is irrigated. The underground water is pumped into the center of the field and is then piped along a long metal arm fitted with spray nozzles. As the arm, driven by motors, slowly travels around and around, water is distributed to all parts of the field by the sprays.

New towns

Some countries are trying to make even more extensive use of underground water. Egypt has one of the fastest growing human populations, and its capital, Cairo, is already the second biggest city in the world. Yet about 96 percent of Egypt is covered by desert, and nearly all the population is crammed into a narrow strip on either side of the Nile, the major source of irrigation

△ Villagers in Sudan are struggling to cultivate crops in ground threatened by the spread of the desert.

▷ Circular wheat fields in Libya, in the Sahara Desert, are shaped by the way the crops are irrigated (inset).

water. In an attempt to relieve the population pressure in the Nile Valley, the Egyptian government is trying to establish a new agricultural district at Farafra in the middle of the desert.

Below Farafra is a vast natural reservoir of fresh water. Deep wells bring this water gushing to the surface at a rate of thousands of gallons per hour. Despite the fact that Egypt is a fairly poor country, the government has invested a considerable amount of money in building modern housing, schools, and hospitals in the Farafra region. By encouraging people to move out into the desert, they hope not only to grow much more food, but also to relieve the overcrowding in Cairo and the Nile Valley.

Running dry?

Wheat fields and new towns represent very ambitious attempts to put the desert to good use. However, many scientists believe that the attempts are also very shortsighted, because the water supply will not last forever. Spray irrigation, such as is used in the wheat fields, is extremely wasteful. Spraying water into the desert air means that large quantities are lost by evaporation before it can soak back into the ground.

Equally important is the fact that the water in the underground reservoirs has slowly accumulated over millions of years. At present it is being removed at a much faster rate than it is being replaced by rainfall. In parts of the Arabian desert, the water table—the depth of the water below the surface—is dropping by a few yards each year. Sooner or later, even the deepest wells will run dry. In Egypt, some experts believe that the Farafra reservoir will only support farming for about 50 years. They argue that persuading large numbers of people to go and live in the desert is only creating a crisis for the future.

The lowering of the water table will not only affect the new agricultural projects. Many oases and springs are also fed by the same underground reservoirs. As these too begin to dry up, settlements hundreds of miles away will be seriously affected, and there will also be less water for natural vegetation and animal wildlife.

The best irrigation methods in the desert will be those that use water sparingly. The most important advance has been the development of trickle and drip irrigation systems. These use plastic piping laid along the ground to deliver very small amounts of water precisely where they are needed most, at the base of the plant above the roots. By delivering water directly to the root system, rather than spraying it into the air, trickle and drip irrigation systems reduce water loss from evaporation to a minimum.

Plastic protection

Greenhouses are a useful way of creating artificial environments. In the desert, greenhouses for plants serve the same purpose as the sealed burrow of a small mammal. Inside the greenhouse, the humidity of the air can be raised much higher than that outside. The increased humidity slows the rate of evaporation, and far less water is needed for irrigation.

The development of greenhouse agriculture in the desert has been greatly boosted by the introduction of modern materials. Plastic sheeting means that

△ Melons are grown in these greenhouses in the Negev Desert in Israel.

greenhouses can be built larger and more cheaply than with glass. A useful side effect of the plastic sheeting is that it rapidly becomes dulled by the effects of the climate. As a result, the sunlight reaching the plants under cultivation is filtered and reduced to a more acceptable level.

Plant engineering

Many desert areas extend right down to the sea, which is a limitless source of water. Unfortunately the process of desalination, converting seawater into fresh water, is extremely difficult on a large scale and uses large amounts of expensive energy. An alternative solution is to breed plants that can grow on a diet of seawater. Scientists in the United States, for example, have developed tomato plants that can be irrigated with salt water.

However, there is a large question mark over this whole area of research. Irrigating the land with seawater will mean that even more salt will build up in the soil. Many coastal desert areas are already too salty for most forms of life. Pumping more salt onto the land may not be the best solution.

Applied ecology

The desert is a very harsh environment and one where even the smallest advantage can make a crucial difference. Part of the purpose of ecology is to learn how these advantages operate. Extensive studies have been made on wild shrubs in the Sahara. The research has shown that more than 90 percent of all seedlings that survive their first summer were found virtually next to the edge of a stone. In one study, only 1 seedling out of more than 400 was more than ½ inch from a stone. The stone provides the seedling with a microclimate where it is cool and shady, and where the rate of evaporation is lower than it is a few inches away.

In parts of the Sahel, workers are now teaching local farmers that stones do not have to be cleared from a field. Instead, the stones can be used to provide their crops with a better start in life.

On a much larger scale, some Australian farmers are now using a related method to bring vegetation back to areas of exposed and hard-baked clay. Bulldozers are used to cut a series of shallow grooves and depressions in the ground, and the rest is left up to nature. These artificial hollows in the clay surface serve as traps for windblown seeds and moisture. The sheltered conditions inside the hollow are often enough to give the seeds the small advantage they need in order to take root and grow naturally.

▽ Acacia seedlings are planted close to stones to help trap water near the roots.